British Library Cataloguing in Publication Data

Lindsay, Frances
    Runaway Bim.
    I. Title   II. Cope, Jane
    823'.914 [J]
    ISBN 0-340-49707-6

Text copyright © Frances Lindsay 1989
Illustrations copyright © Hodder and Stoughton Ltd 1989

First published 1989

Published by Hodder and Stoughton Children's Books,
a division of Hodder and Stoughton Ltd,
Mill Road, Dunton Green, Sevenoaks, Kent TN13 2YA

Photoset by En to En, Tunbridge Wells, Kent

Printed in Great Britain by T. J. Press (Padstow) Ltd,
Padstow, Cornwall

ROOSTERS

FRANCES LINDSAY

Runaway Bim

illustrated by
Jane Cope

HODDER AND STOUGHTON
London   Sydney   Auckland   Toronto

1 **Unwanted**

Bim waited impatiently for Toby and his
new friend to come home from school.
Toby had been talking about Richard for
days, saying how clever he was,
and because Toby admired him so much
Bim could hardly wait to see him.

At last they came and Bim, peeping
through the banisters, saw a fair-haired
boy, bigger than Toby. He looked far too

tidy, and was wiping his feet carefully on the mat. Toby's mum liked him on sight but Jemma, stuffing her coat untidily into the cupboard, whispered to Beth, 'Show-off!'

Bim went upstairs. He looked out of the window and thought of the day Toby had bought him from Mr Totty's toy shop. There had been great excitement when Toby and his sisters had discovered that the toy koala could talk and do magical things. Somehow they had managed to keep it a secret from everyone and Bim had taken great care to be just a toy when anyone else was about.

After tea, the boys came into Toby's room to look at his collection of matchbox labels. Richard couldn't take his eyes off Bim. Then he started laughing. 'A toy koala on your bed!' he chortled.

Toby flushed. 'You mean old Bim.'

'Is that what you call it? A stupid name

for a stupid toy. I gave up things like that
ages ago. Don't have pets either. It's too
sissy for words. As for having it on your
bed . . .'

He sounded disgusted and Toby looked
away. 'I expect my little sister Beth put
him there,' he whispered, hoping that Bim
would not hear what he said.

Richard went soon afterwards, leaving Toby feeling cross with Bim for showing him up in front of Richard and Bim upset by what had been said. He tried to talk about it at bedtime but Toby wouldn't answer and after reading for a while he put out the light.

Bim waited for him to say 'Hop in' as he always did but he didn't say anything, and after a while Bim climbed into bed and snuggled down under the blankets.

'You're taking up all the room,' Toby grumbled, and pushed Bim on to the floor.

9

The little koala could not believe what was happening. 'But . . . but I always sleep in your bed,' he said.

There was no answer and Bim spent an unhappy night on the window-sill.

The next day, Toby and Jemma made some toffee. Bim wanted to help but he kept getting in the way. 'You're a nuisance, Bim,' Toby said. 'Buzz off!'

The toffee smelt so delicious that Bim could not resist dipping a paw in it.
'Oh, oh, oh!' he shouted. 'I've burnt myself.'
'It serves you right. Don't you know it's stupid to touch anything hot?' said Toby.

Jemma was kinder. 'Put your paw under the cold-water tap, Bim. It'll take away the pain.'

Bim did so, then licked his paw. 'Yummy yum! It tastes lovely. I think it might be taking away a teeny-weeny bit of the pain.'

'Buzz off!' Toby said again.

Bim went upstairs. Beth was dressing her favourite doll. 'Why is Abigail wearing her best dress?' he asked. 'It's not Sunday.'

'I know it isn't but Mrs Baxter said we can take a toy or a book to school tomorrow so I'm getting Abigail ready.'

'P'rhaps Toby will take me.' Bim said hopefully and hurried away to clean his teeth, put on his best bow tie, and stuff a bag of his favourite peppermint toffees in the pocket of his dungarees.

As soon as Toby came into the bedroom, Bim asked if he could go to school with him the next day.

'No, you can't!' said Toby.

'Why not? Beth's taking Abigail.'

'It's different for Beth, she's in the Infants. Big boys don't take toys to school.'

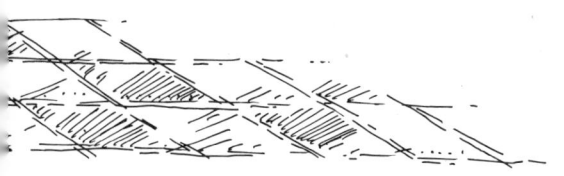

'No one need know. I could hide in your satchel.'

'You're not coming! I don't want you,' Toby said angrily.

He hardly spoke to Bim during the next two days and poor Bim sat alone at night in a corner of the bedroom, crying bitterly. He couldn't think what he had done to upset his best friend or why Toby didn't want him any more, but if he didn't then the time had come for Bim to leave home.

He told himself he would try to think of it as an adventure, but as he packed his spare pair of dungarees, his toothbrush and a bag of peppermint toffees it was hard to stop the tears from falling, and he went away leaving his best bow tie behind . . .

2 Hiding Place

Toby worried about Bim all the way to school. He knew he had been unkind and he was ashamed of the way he had treated him. If only Richard hadn't said it was sissy to have toys and pets . . . if only he wasn't always so right . . . if only . . .

But Toby came home much happier, with the exciting news that he had been chosen to captain a team in a quiz on wildlife. 'It's in a week's time. Bim's going to be our mascot. Henry wanted to bring his rabbit and Steven his dog, there are three of us in the team you see, but Sir said my toy koala would be better.'

'Who's in the other team?' Beth asked.

'Fiona Watts and Sarah Marsh. Richard's the captain.'

'That's not fair!' Jemma cried. 'It ought to be a girl.'

'It was to have been his sister, Joanna, but she's got chicken-pox so the girls chose Richard instead because he's so clever and they're determined to win. He doesn't believe in mascots. He's always on about it being babyish to keep toys but Mr Harding said that was nonsense. We're never too old.'

'Of course you're not! Your gran's still got old Tim, her teddy-bear, and Beth's got the doll your mum had when she was little,' said Dad.

Toby raced off to tell Bim the news and say he was sorry he had treated him so badly. But Bim was not to be found and, although Toby and the girls searched everywhere, when bedtime came the little koala was still missing . . .

But Bim had not travelled further than the big hollow tree in the overgrown garden next door. He went inside and curled up on a pile of twigs and leaves, to see how comfortable it was.

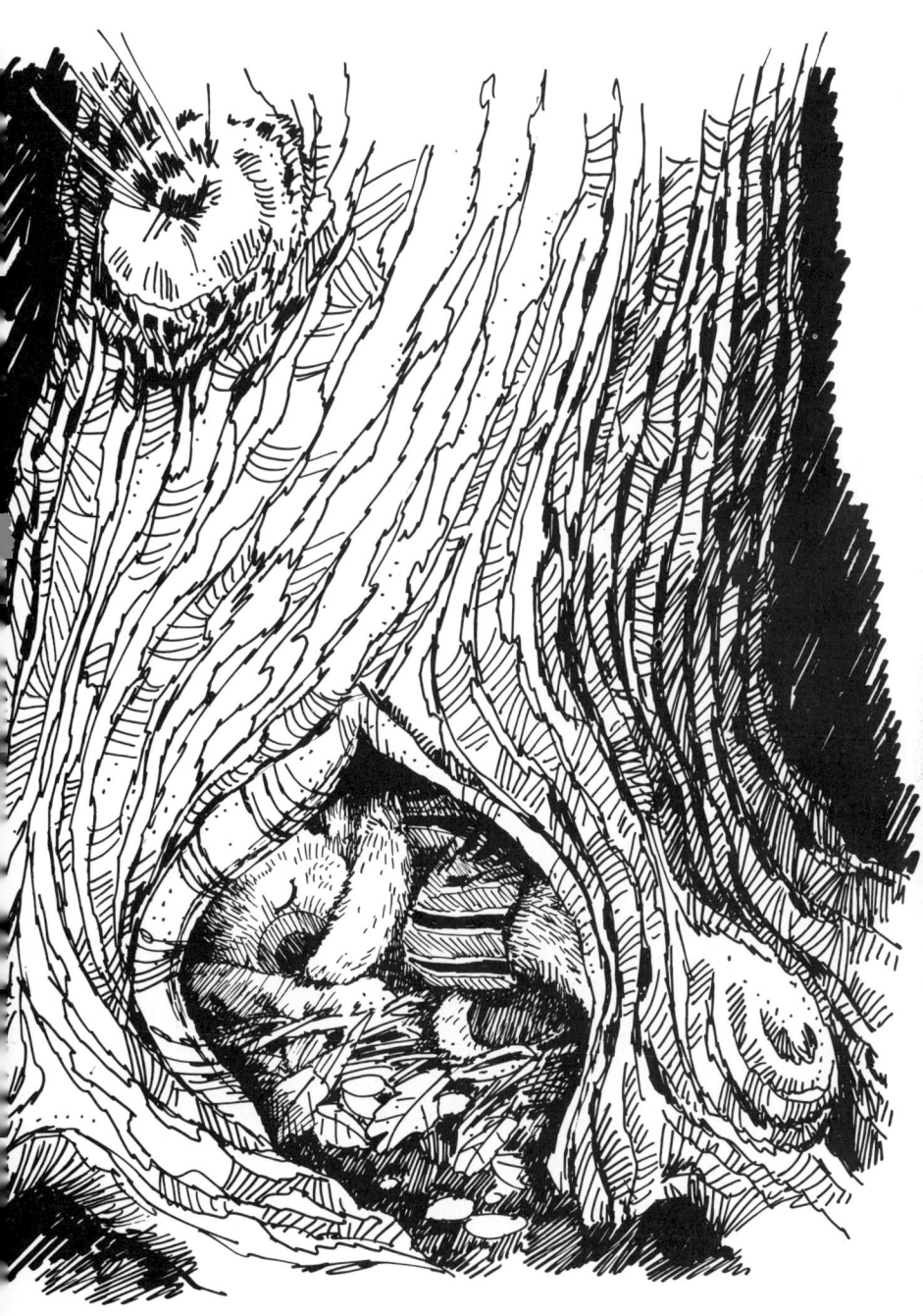

The house had been empty ever since old Mrs Jones had gone into hospital. The tree would be his new home and, although it wasn't very comfortable, at least he would be able to watch over his young friends and make sure nothing happened to them.

He waited to see them safely home from school, then went to the bottom of the road to visit Lazybones and her new kittens, so he did not hear Toby and the girls calling him.

The kittens had grown a lot since Bim
had last seen them and they were chasing
each other round the warm shed where
they had been born.

Lazybones wanted to go out and she asked Bim to babysit for her. He was pleased. He didn't like being on his own and the shed was more comfortable than the hollow tree. In the end he stayed the night and did not return until the children were home from school the next day.

When he saw they were all right he went back to the shed, and again stayed the night. Warmed by the kittens who crowded close to him, Bim slept late.

When he got back to the tree he found his toothbrush, his spare pair of dungarees and what was left of the toffees scattered on the ground. A squirrel was busy with the pile of twigs.

'What d'you think you're doing?
Bim asked.

'What does it look like?' the squirrel
said rudely. 'The wind blew my drey down
so I'm collecting more sticks to build
another.'

'Your what?'

'My drey . . . my nest. Don't you know
anything?'

Bim did not answer and the squirrel
went on:

'There's no room for you here!'
and disappeared inside the tree.

That's not very friendly, Bim thought.
He picked up his belongings, knowing he
must look for a new home. He could go
back to the kittens – they would be
pleased to have him – but he wanted to
be near Toby. He found a dry place under
some bushes and stayed there, wondering
where he could live now Toby didn't want
him any more.

3 Accident!

Because he had been spending so much time with Lazybones' family, Bim had no idea that the children had been searching high and low for him. They had turned out cupboards, looked under the beds and on top of wardrobes and pried into every corner of the garden. Toby had climbed the apple tree, hoping to find him there, but still there was no sign of Bim.

'I think he's been stolen,' said Jemma.

'I think he's run away,' said Beth.

'Don't be silly!' Toby snapped. He knew it was his fault if Bim had done so and he was afraid he would never see him again.

Early next morning, Bim heard Beth crying. He climbed the drainpipe and peeped into her bedroom window.

The first thing he saw was the goldfish lying on its side on top of the water and he knew it was dead.

'You must give Goldie a proper funeral,' said Toby.

'You can have that pretty pink box, the one I had for Christmas. It will make a lovely coffin and it still smells of scented soap,' Jemma said.

Beth gave a watery smile. 'We must put some cotton-wool in first.'

'After breakfast, you can chose a spot for Goldie's grave and I'll dig it for you,' Toby promised.

Bim did not wait to hear more but ran into Mrs Jones garden to find a place from where he could watch everything. In his eagerness he did not look where he was going, and before he knew what was happening he tripped and was falling down . . . down . . . down . . .

It seemed a long while before he could think clearly. Every bit of him ached and the small patch of blue sky far above showed him he would never get out of the hole he was in without help. His magic was just not strong enough to do it by himself. He took a deep breath and began calling, 'Help . . . Help . . . Help . . .'

After a while the children came into the garden. Beth carried the pink box, Jemma some forget-me-nots, and Toby a spade.

They went twice round the garden before Beth chose a patch of earth under the apple tree and Goldie was buried.

The children said a little prayer, put the flowers on the grave, and hunted for pebbles to decorate it.

'There are heaps of lovely round ones in the garden next door. Mrs Jones had them all along the path.'

'I know, Beth, but we're not allowed to go in there and even if we were we'd never get through that prickly hedge,' Jemma sighed.

'I could. I'm smaller than either of you,' Beth answered.

'Well . . . if you're very careful,' Toby said doubtfully, 'but you'll need something to put the pebbles in.'

'Use this flowerpot,' said Jemma.

They went along the untidy hedge until they found an opening big enough for Beth to squeeze through.

The squirrel, disturbed by all the noise this made, ran off chattering angrily as Beth called, 'I can see the pebbles but there are lots of stinging nettles and prickly bits.'

It was then that she heard a faint cry
and although she was scared she stood
still, listening as it came again. Hurrying
as fast as she dared, she came upon a
well, half-hidden in the undergrowth.
She looked down and saw Bim huddled at
the bottom.

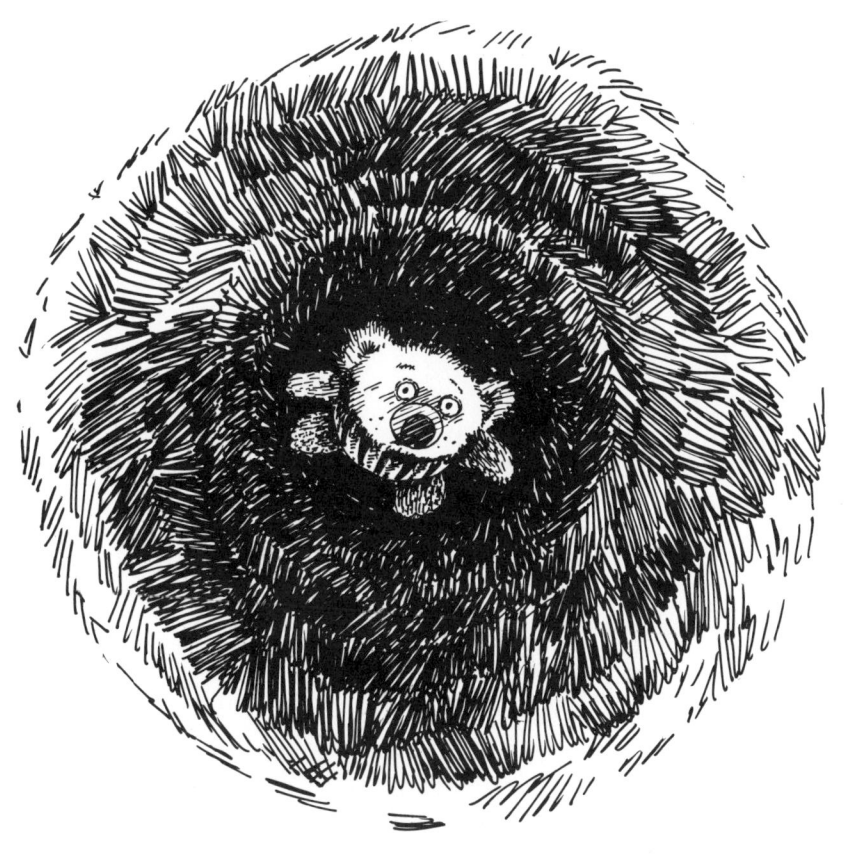

'Bim . . . Bim . . . It's me, Beth. Thank goodness I've found you. Are you all right?'

'N . . . not really. I . . . I want to go home,' he sobbed.

'Of course you do. I'll get Toby. He'll soon have you out of there.'

Her excited cries brought Toby with a rope and, forcing his way through the hedge, he lowered it carefully into the well. 'I've made a noose in it, Bim. Slip it round your waist and I'll haul you up. Don't be afraid, you'll be quite safe.'

Bim did as he was told and was pulled gently to the top and although he was wet and dirty the children couldn't stop hugging him. 'Thank goodness you're safe, Bim. I thought I'd lost you for ever,' Toby cried.

'You saved my life, you and Beth. You're heroes.'

'And you're the bravest koala that ever was . . .'

4 Nature Quiz

The pebbles forgotten, they went indoors.

'I see you've found Bim. Where was he?'
Mum asked.

'Out there,' Toby said vaguely.

'You should take more care of your toys,'
she said crossly.

'I'm going to take more care of you, Bim,'
Toby whispered. 'And guess what! We're
having a quiz at school, just our class,
and you're going to be my team's mascot.'

Bim's eyes were like stars. 'Will I go to
school with you?'

'Of course you will but you'll have to be
a proper toy koala. No one must guess
you're magic.'

When bedtime came and the light was out, Toby said, 'I know it was my fault you ran away. I'm sorry I was beastly to you, Bim.'

'I've forgotten all about it,' he answered and nestled closer to Toby.

Toby spent the weekend trying to remember all he had learnt about birds and animals and insects and hoping he would be asked questions he could answer. After tea on Sunday the family gathered round the table and fired questions at him until bedtime. Upstairs, as goodnights were being said, Bim asked what a squirrel's nest was called and chuckled when none of the children knew.

'It's a drey,' he said.

'I don't believe it. You're making it up.'

'No I'm not, Toby. It really is a drey.'

'I used to like squirrels until they ate Grandma's tulip bulbs,' said Jemma.

'I don't like them because they eat the bread we put out for the birds. They're greedy things,' Beth said.

Bim wore his best bow tie to school. Toby's friends said he looked a winner and Sir was sure Bim would make a great mascot.

Fiona and Sarah had brought mascots of their own, a woolly rabbit called Nibbles and a shabby teddy-bear called Sam. Richard was cross. 'They're a load of rubbish like good-luck charms,' he grumbled.

The class cheered as the teams took their places and the quiz began. Questions and answers came fast:

'What is a fawn?'

'A young deer.'

'What is a cygnet?'

'A young swan.'

'What is a fox's tail called?'

'A brush.'

'What is a rabbit's?'

'A scut.'

'How many eggs does a blackbird lay?'

'Three to five, usually.'

As the questions went on it was plain to see there was nothing to choose between the teams; either could be the winner.

The last three questions came:

'What is a fox's hole called?'

'An earth,' said Richard.

'What is a badger's burrow called?'

'A sett,' said Toby.

'What is a squirrel's nest called?'

Richard looked helplessly at Fiona and Sarah who shook their heads. Mr Harding turned to Toby:

'What is a squirrel's nest called?'

'A drey!' Toby shouted, and the class cheered and clapped the winners by one point.

'We'd have won if the girls hadn't brought those stupid mascots,' Richard grumbled.

'We won *because* Bim was our mascot,' laughed Toby.

On the way home Jemma said, 'Henry told me you were a wizard mascot, Bim. He said you were really magical.'

'If only he knew,' Beth giggled.

'It's true, you were a wizard mascot, Bim. I wouldn't have known the answer to that last question if you hadn't helped me.'

'That's what best friends are for,' said Bim . . .